MARIE-JOSÉE THIBAULT

2

THE HOLY POPE
Saint John Paul II
SPEAKS

The Holy Pope Saint John Paul II Speaks - Book 2

Published by Abba Books LLC
abbabooksllc@gmail.com
Copyright © 2023 Marie-Josée Thibault

All Rights Reserved

No part of this publication may be reproduced, distributed, or transmitted in any form or by any means, including photocopying, recording, or other electronic or mechanical methods, without the prior written permission of the publisher.

First Edition, 2023
Designed and Edited by Abba Books LLC
ISBN: 979-8-9887805-7-1

Abba Books LLC
34972 Newark Blvd, #441
Newark, CA 94560

www.abbamyfatheriloveyou.com
https://www.facebook.com/AbbaILoveYouBooks/

Thy Peace on Earth must be achieved. No light, no litany must be spared to honor Thy Grace.
-Saint Paul

CONTENTS

Preface	VI	Chap 11	29	Chap 22	59
Chap 1	1	Chap 12	31	Chap 23	63
Chap 2	5	Chap 13	33	Chap 24	65
Chap 3	9	Chap 14	35	Chap 25	67
Chap 4	11	Chap 15	37	Chap 26	73
Chap 5	13	Chap 16	41	Chap 27	77
Chap 6	17	Chap 17	43	Chap 28	81
Chap 7	19	Chap 18	45	Chap 29	83
Chap 8	21	Chap 19	47	Chap 30	87
Chap 9	23	Chap 20	51	Chap 31	93
Chap 10	25	Chap 21	57	Chap 32	95
				Chap 33	97
				Chap 34	101
				Chap 35	105
				Chap 36	111
				Chap 37	115
				Chap 38	117

PREFACE

I have been regularly blessed with visitations from Saint John Paul II over the past few years. He typically shows up on Friday or Saturday mornings and appears in my living room next to my Marian shrine. We speak, discuss, and pray together, and then he disappears. He is my spiritual director: He follows my progress and instructs me, gives me encouragement when I feel overwhelmed, scolds me when I deserve it, explains things I fail to understand, and—above all—blesses me. Lastly, he ordered me to publish these messages to humanity.

"I say unto you, I say unto you verily: God loves you, and He has assigned your soul to me in order for me to take it to Him as rapidly as possible through the Holy Name of Jesus Christ and the ever-Immaculate Heart of Mary. Your soul is in my hands. At this time, you are reading these lines, and it will be here forever and ever."

Amid the noise of modern times, Saint John Paul II's unwavering and heavenly voice rises like a timeless song, inviting us to a totally different rhythm. This book offers you the unique opportunity to dwell in the mystical presence of a visionary saint whose words, actions, and spirit are more relevant today than they were while he was alive. As you flip through these pages, be prepared to engage with Saint John Paul II himself—allow the eternal spirit of the saint to guide you on a path of intimate companionship, mystical bonding, and holy transformation.

Make sure not to miss Books 1 and 2.

Saint John Paul II, I love you!

Marie-Josée

THE HOLY POPE SPEAKS: Saint John Paul II

My children, today I want to speak to you about the future on earth. Events that lie ahead will be difficult and intense for all inhabitants of planet earth, without exception. These events, allowed by God Himself, aim at testing the hearts of God's children, each and every one of you.

Why? For God has decided so. Why are you asking me again? This mystery that is the Will of God concerning all things is a mystery that we must share in communion with one another, all of us His children, on earth as in Heaven. The universal cycles of growth and decay, generation and destruction, life and death are independent of our scope and our understanding. It is sufficient to say, at this time, that what is approaching is not the result of chance or of demonic ideas that will strike the earth.

THE HOLY POPE SPEAKS: Saint John Paul II

What is approaching has been viewed and permitted by God, even if it is true that demonic forces will be behind the tragic events affecting everyone. God, in His Divine Wisdom, decides this or that, utilizing the destructive goals of the devil if it is so according to His Will, in order to test the merits of your hearts and the uprightness of your decisions in the face of adversity. And the adversity will be great, I am sorry to announce...

Alleluia! Alleluia! Alleluia!
Blessed is he who keeps his heart
wide open for God only, now and forever,
for God Himself shall relieve him.

J ✝✝✝✝✝ PII

THE HOLY POPE SPEAKS: Saint John Paul II

My children, I am delighted to walk among you on earth. Yes, my children, using my Etheric body, cherished and given by God, I have the ability to travel as I please, here and there, in your houses, on the street, in your vehicles, on an aircraft (I liked to travel by plane at the time), or in any structure of any kind on earth.

In addition, my Etheric body knows no limits of time and space; thus I am able to be present, attentive, and to perform miracles in the Name of God the Father Almighty in several thousand locations simultaneously on earth.

I know that this concept is difficult for you to understand at this time. Be not afraid! Pray, pray, pray, my children, and my Holiness will follow you wherever you go.

Alleluia! Alleluia! Alleluia!
Blessed is he who prays and seeks the intercession
of Saint John Paul II, in the Name of the Father
Almighty, for my Holiness will accompany him
until the end of his life—and beyond.

Amen.
Alleluia!

THE HOLY POPE SPEAKS: Saint John Paul II

My children, always remain in the Presence of my Holiness within the Light of Christ! Know that my Presence near you is, as of today, made Permanent, Ineffable, and Miraculous, by virtue of the Cosmic Powers enclosed in this book blessed by God!

I am there; I will always be there, today, tomorrow, and the rest of your life, and for eternity!

Amen. Alleluia!

THE HOLY POPE SPEAKS: Saint John Paul II

My children,
I am capable of performing miracles for you now by virtue of my Holiness granted by God the Father Almighty. Pray! Pray! Pray! And your prayers will be granted!

Pray this way: "Saint John Paul II, intercede for me, before God the Father Almighty, for the obtention of [requested favor], by virtue of your Gift of Compassion and of Holiness, through the Holy and Glorious Light of our Lord Jesus Christ and the Immaculate Heart of Mary. Amen. So be it."

My duty here in Heaven is to work very hard with Christ Jesus, the Light of the world, and Saint Paul the Apostle, the Logos of conversion to Christ Jesus, so to illuminate the entire world and allow everyone to enter the Legion of Saint Paul.

For the Legion of Saint Paul is part of the Great Plan of Salvation for humanity according to the Will of the Absolute Father. Your soul, dear reader, is in my hands, and I personally invite you to join the Legion of Saint Paul.

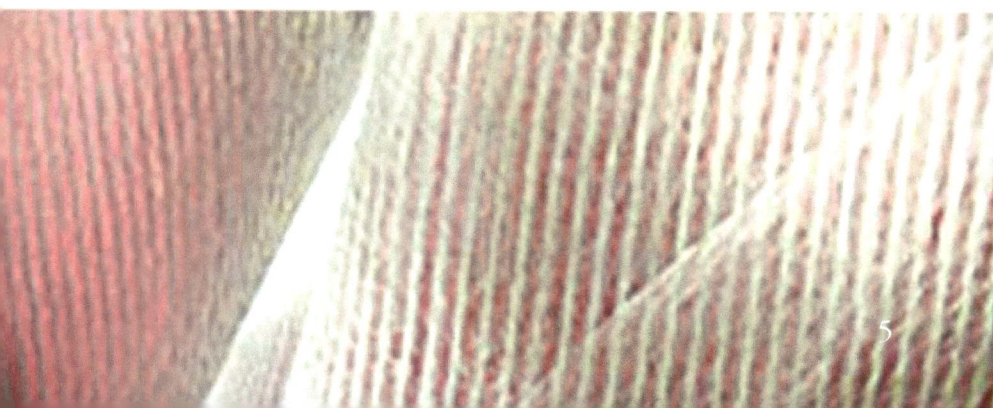

THE HOLY POPE SPEAKS: Saint John Paul II

For the Legion of Saint Paul has earned the Mercy of God the Father Almighty by virtue of the Powers won by the cosmic work of redemption of the five crosses.

Alleluia! Alleluia! Alleluia!
Blessed are those who are invited to join
the Legion of Saint Paul,
for the Legion of Saint Paul will see
the New Sun that will rise shortly.

THE HOLY POPE SPEAKS — Saint John Paul II

My children, I am there in front of you as you are reading these Lines. My Holiness has joined with your humanity, through the Glory, the Name, and the bleeding and triumphant Wounds of our Lord Jesus Christ. I am delighted and I am fulfilled to participate in the edification and the salvation of your soul blessed by God.

Alleluia! Alleluia! Alleluia!
Blessed is he who receives the visitation
from Saint John Paul II,
for Holiness has entered into his life.

Amen. Alleluia!

My children, I am capable of performing miracles for you now by virtue of my Holiness granted by God the Father Almighty. Pray! Pray! Pray! And your prayers will be granted!

~ Saint John Paul II

THE HOLY POPE SPEAKS — Saint John Paul II

My children, I am among you and I am also merging with your Energetic bodies. You see, your body, created by God, is fluid and permeable to the influx of Energy originating from the rest of the universe. Be very firm in your conviction that my Presence with you is taking place around you and through you, thus allowing me to read your mind, capture the emotions of your heart, and inspire you on your path to Holiness. For I, Saint John Paul II, promise you today to render you Holy in the Eyes of God.

Alleluia! Alleluia! Alleluia!
Blessed is he who opens his heart very wide
to the Holiness offered today by God Himself.

Amen. Alleluia!

J ✝✝✝✝✝ P II

THE HOLY POPE SPEAKS: Saint John Paul II

My children,
I am particularly delighted to meet you, you who are reading me. Despite the fact that I am entering energetically into your life at this time through these Lines blessed by God, I have visited you on several occasions in the past. Your life, your joys, your sorrows, your dreams, your disappointments: I know them all.

I, Saint John Paul II, the Pope who became Holy by the Infinite Grace of God the Father Almighty, love you already and I have loved you since a long time ago. I am with you now and for the rest of your life—and beyond. I will never abandon you; I will always assist you; I am preparing a path of Holiness for you that will take you directly into the loving Arms of God through the Light of Christ the Savior.

Alleluia! Alleluia! Alleluia!
Blessed are those invited to the Kingdom of God,
for I, Saint John Paul II, will welcome them
at the Gates of the Kingdom
after the passage that is death.

Amen. Alleluia!

THE HOLY POPE SPEAKS: Saint John Paul II

My children,
I am pleased to participate in the edification of your soul, for God the Father Almighty has decided so. You, dear reader, dear beloved heart, dear soul blessed by God, my precious friend on suffering earth, have become today a member of the Legion of Saint Paul.

The Legion of Saint Paul holds, in the Eyes of God, all the Infinite Mercy that He pours forth over humankind, by virtue of the meritorious work earned by the nobility of the five crosses. We will continue our study of the Legion of Saint Paul later in this book.

*For now, rejoice, as Saint John Paul II,
your Benefactor in Heaven,
beholds you and loves you so much!
I am Saint John Paul II and I love you so much!*

Amen. Alleluia!

THE HOLY POPE SPEAKS — Saint John Paul II

My children,
I speak to you today with a serious tone. The events that lie ahead will be more intense, more dramatic, and more global than you can imagine. Never in history has taken place what is being prepared before you and what you will have to confront.

Your prayers today appease the Justice of the Living God. Your prayers tomorrow will continue to appease Divine Justice. However, the Decision of God the Father has already been made, and the Great Day of Purification is moving rapidly toward the earth. Pray my children, pray today, for Divine Justice will soon be reaching your door.

*Alleluia! Alleluia! Alleluia!
Blessed is he who prays today,
for tomorrow belongs to God.*

Amen. Alleluia!

THE HOLY POPE SPEAKS: Saint John Paul II

My children,
I am disappointed to witness such weariness, such negligence, and such indifference vis-à-vis our Savior, our Lord Jesus Christ. This attitude, which I observed during my Papacy, grows and infiltrates among more and more human souls, even among the Catholic people. Such a grave mistake! Such a waste of virtue! So much time lost in the path toward God!

For the minutes are numbered which will bring us to the Great Day of Purification of God, when every thought, every emotion, and every action will be carefully reviewed and assessed by God the Father Almighty.

His Justice is infallible and His Mercy is gentle according to the merits or the offenses written in the Great Book of Life that exists concerning every soul living on earth. For the life you have been given belongs to the Father and takes place within Him, for Him, and through Him, our Supreme Creator.

Alleluia! Alleluia! Alleluia!
Blessed is he who loves God
and prays to God today,
for today his Book of Life says so.

Amen. Alleluia!

No Light nor Litany Must be Spared

Christ in the Carpenter's Shop

to Honor thy Grace

THE HOLY POPE SPEAKS: Saint John Paul II

My children,
I am particularly saddened to notice the lack of discipline with regard to the practice of religious precepts as taught by the Catholic Church. Daily rituals, carried out either in the privacy of your home or at church, are fundamental to the health of the soul and your protection against the assaults of the enemy.

Study the fundamental principles of the Catholic religion, put into practice the simple prayers of love and gratitude for the Holy Trinity, say your rosary every day, and contemplate and meditate on Christ crucified by us.

I say unto you, I say unto you verily, God the Father Almighty rejoices in the soul adopting an inner discipline of respect and devotion before the Sacred and the Divine He has created.

*Alleluia! Alleluia! Alleluia!
Blessed is the soul in a state of grace before God
for God Himself will bless this soul.*

Amen. Alleluia!

THE HOLY POPE SPEAKS Saint John Paul II

My children, I am here in Paradise, near Christ Jesus, my Master and my Savior, and I am also very close to Saint Paul the Apostle.

Saint Paul the Apostle is the leader of the Legion of Saint Paul on earth as in Heaven. The Legion of Saint Paul has earned the Infinite Divine Mercy by virtue of the merits accomplished by the lineage of Saint Paul on earth. The lineage of Saint Paul represents a fundamental concept of the Teaching of Saint Paul that you will find in one of His books, entitled *I Am Saint Paul the Apostle.*

The Logos of Saint Paul the Apostle represents the Logos of conversion to Christ Jesus, our Savior and our God. The Father Almighty wishes to see all souls on earth converting to Christ Jesus, our Everything, His Only Son. I hasten to add here that in Paradise, all the pure Souls and all the Saints are praying and are already part of the Legion of Saint Paul.

My role in the Legion of Saint Paul is very important and I thank God the Father Almighty. We will speak again of the Legion of Saint Paul later on. For the moment, let us give thanks to this glorious and fearless Apostle who has accomplished His mission to perfection, according to the command of God the Father and for the Love of Christ.

Alleluia! Alleluia! Alleluia!
Blessed are the members of the Legion of Saint Paul
on earth as in Heaven. Amen! Alleluia!

13
THE HOLY POPE SPEAKS — Saint John Paul II

My children, be assured of my miraculous help and my permanent assistance at your side. God the Father Almighty gave me complete freedom to do everything possible to ensure your path of redemption and, more particularly, your path of Holiness. For your soul is precious in His Sovereign Eyes!

Alleluia! Alleluia! Alleluia!
Blessed is he who walks
in the path of redemption and Holiness
with Saint John Paul II at his side.

Amen. Alleluia!

THE HOLY POPE SPEAKS: Saint John Paul II

My children,
I was born among men to become Pope. I died among men to become Holy. Such was the desire of God the Father Almighty for me, Karol Wojtyla, a servant of God.

My Holy Name is now Saint John Paul II, for I was baptized here in Paradise by the Hands of Saint John the Baptist, the Master of Cosmic Baptism, according to the Supreme Will of God the Father. Saint John the Baptist is a Great Master of the Major Mysteries of the Creation, for God has decided so, at the beginning of the Creation, the Cosmic Genesis.

Alleluia! Alleluia! Alleluia!
Blessed are the souls invited to Cosmic Baptism
by the Holy Hands of Saint John the Baptist,
the Master of Holiness in Heaven.

Amen. Alleluia!

THE HOLY POPE SPEAKS Saint John Paul II

My children, I am among the Holy Nation in Heaven, for God the Father Almighty has decided so.

Here, in Paradise, from where I speak to you today, the Saints in Paradise are working ceaselessly for the salvation of humanity, under the leadership of Saint Paul the Apostle, the Emissary of Christ on earth as in Heaven.

Saint Paul the Apostle, through His work on earth and His current work in Paradise, contributes to the conversion of your soul to Christ Jesus. Indeed, the Logos of Saint Paul the Apostle, present in all human hearts, holds the key to the comprehension of the Teachings of Christ Jesus. Without Him, without Saint Paul the Apostle, your heart would be spiritually impoverished in ways indescribable.

*Alleluia! Alleluia! Alleluia! Blessed is he who prays
and who reveres the Sacred Teachings
of Saint Paul the Apostle,
the Logos of conversion to Christ.*

Amen. Alleluia!

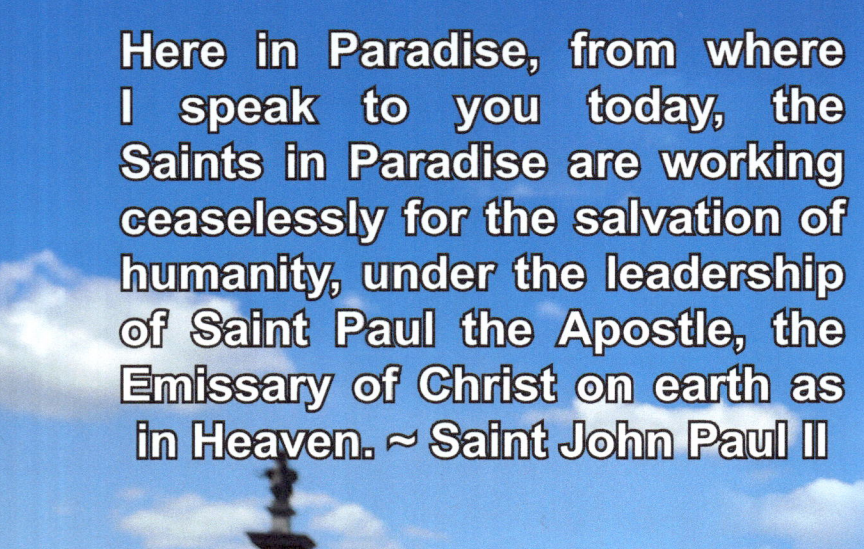

Here in Paradise, from where I speak to you today, the Saints in Paradise are working ceaselessly for the salvation of humanity, under the leadership of Saint Paul the Apostle, the Emissary of Christ on earth as in Heaven. ~ Saint John Paul II

THE HOLY POPE SPEAKS — Saint John Paul II

My children, Christ Jesus is unable to execute your path of redemption on your behalf despite all His Universal Power. Your consent, your initiatives, your dedication, your efforts, are necessary at the beginning of the awakening of Consciousness and all along your Spiritual journey.

Christ Jesus, by Himself and through us, the Saints in Paradise and the Angels of God, will assist you at every moment of your life on earth. For we are your Benefactors, assigned to the well-being and the salvation of your soul by God the Father Himself.

Alleluia! Alleluia! Alleluia!
Blessed be the Christ,
the Light of the world
and the Light of your life!

Amen. Alleluia!

THE HOLY POPE SPEAKS — Saint John Paul II

My children, Christ Jesus, our Universal Savior, our Absolute Master, our Sovereign toward everything, today has taken a decisive step inside your life, dear beloved reader.

For as of today, the salvation of your soul has been initiated, by the means of this book blessed by God and through my Sacred Words chosen by God Himself. For I, Saint John Paul II, a servant of God, an Apostle of Christ, a Friend of Saint Paul the Apostle, unite with you forever in a Grand Gesture of the Infinite Mercy of God the Loving Father.

> *I say unto you, I say unto you verily,*
> *I, Saint John Paul II,*
> *I walk in the Light of Christ in Heaven,*
> *and I walk in the Light of Christ on earth,*
> *now and forever.*

Amen. Alleluia!

THE HOLY POPE SPEAKS — Saint John Paul II

My children, be pure in your thoughts and be charitable in your heart. God the Father Almighty knows the deepest recesses of your mind and every nuance of your emotions. For He is the Source of all life and of all matter, on earth as in Heaven, and in all dimensions of the universe, known and unknown to man.

Never doubt the total and permanent perception of all your thoughts, your emotions, your words, your actions and your works from God, even if it seems impossible to comprehend by human understanding.

I say unto you, I say unto you verily, God sees everything, hears everything, and feels everything that you are experiencing, each and every one of you.

Alleluia! Alleluia! Alleluia!
Glory to God in the Highest Heaven
and on earth peace to men of good will.

Amen. Alleluia!

19

THE HOLY POPE SPEAKS — Saint John Paul II

My children, I am now able and ready to talk about the events that lie ahead. I pray for you at this time, at this moment that you are reading these Lines, in order to give you strength and faith in God, and that you might remain centered and in interior recollection.

Events that lie ahead will be atrocious. These events will take the shape of a world war. In addition, there will be many unusual events on earth because the dark forces will be more active, and I imply here that their evil actions and their physical visibility will be mounting—until such time that they are all eliminated. Indeed, these enemy forces will eventually be completely decimated by the White Forces of God. However, the tragedies, the barbarities, the cruelties, the suffering generated in the interim will be immense—more than I dare to think.

THE HOLY POPE SPEAKS Saint John Paul II

Remember that God's Great Plan of Salvation implies a direct and visible confrontation between the White Forces and the dark forces before the Definitive and Glorious Triumph of God's Army. For the Decision of the victory belongs to God—of course.

Why the advent of so much suffering and tears on earth? The following pages explain God's Plan of Salvation.

Be strong, my children, remember the Love of God for all His children. I love you and I bless you in the Name of the Father, and of the Son, and of the Holy Spirit.

Amen. Alleluia!

J ✝ ✝ ✝ ✝ ✝ PII

THE HOLY POPE SPEAKS: Saint John Paul II

My children, be strong and be confident in the outcome of the approaching war. God and His Army of Heaven will be victorious, of course, for victory has already been manifested in other dimensions of the universe unknown to man.

Be strong and confident, therefore, for nothing that lies ahead is the result of coincidence or of human ill will. This battle between the White Forces of God and the dark forces of satan is taking place constantly at every moment of the day and night in the invisible dimensions of the universe. This battle will intensify and will materialize among humans in a tragic and global way—inevitably.

There is no victory without battle, and there is no battle without victory.

I say unto you, I say unto you verily, and I repeat it unto you: the looming war is necessary *for it has been ordained by God*. And according to the same Divine Will, this war will be crowned with a Glorious Victory from God, *for it has been ordained by God*.

THE HOLY POPE SPEAKS: Saint John Paul II

The debts toward God are enormous on behalf of humanity, the forces of the devil are rampant, and the cosmic calendar is in place: God the Father Almighty's Great Day of Purification is on our doorstep. After this Great Day of Purification will come Thousands of Days of Peace, Joy, and Harmony on earth, bathed in Christic Light, kindled by the Fire of Love of the Holy Spirit, and always conforming to the Will of the Father. This will be the Age of the New Sun.

*Alleluia! Alleluia! Alleluia!
Blessed is he who prays to God the Father today,
as this one will see the New Sun.*

Amen. Alleluia!

J †††††PII

Alleluia! Alleluia! Alleluia! Blessed is he who prays to God the Father today, as this one will see the New Sun. Amen. Alleluia!
~Saint John Paul II

THE HOLY POPE SPEAKS — Saint John Paul II

My children, My children, I am sorrowful in advance of the horror that will befall the earth. You cannot imagine the cruelty and the perfidy of satan. His demonic soldiers will deploy all their powers in order to create chaos, barbarism, and injustice, as well as suffering on all levels.

Be not afraid! We must pray, pray, pray today, and your prayers will protect you as of today and every day until the rise of the New Sun.

*Alleluia! Alleluia! Alleluia!
Blessed is he who prays today,
for this one is chosen by God
and shall not suffer.*

Amen, Alleluia!

THE HOLY POPE SPEAKS — Saint John Paul II

My children,

I am delighted today to be able to provide clear and precise instructions in anticipation of events ahead.

First, I wish to remind you that no matter what will affect the world, your city, your neighborhood, your home, your family, your friends, or yourself, you must remain calm. By this, I wish to teach you the mental and emotional control through which you can display the necessary effort to stay calm. Then, if not immediately, you must call God: "O God, come to my aid, O Lord, make haste to help me!" This short invocation is very powerful and I encourage you to repeat this prayer several times a day, as of today and every time a difficult situation arises.

Then, I would like you to begin as of now to pray several times a day these important prayers to God: the Lord's Prayer, the Hail Mary, the Creed, and the Jesus Prayer ("Lord Jesus, Son of the Living God, have pity on me, a poor sinner").

In addition, saying a rosary every day represents a Cosmic Force that you are gaining and that is much stronger than you can imagine.

Alleluia! Alleluia! Alleluia! Blessed is he who prays now, for now the Kingdom of Heaven awaits him.

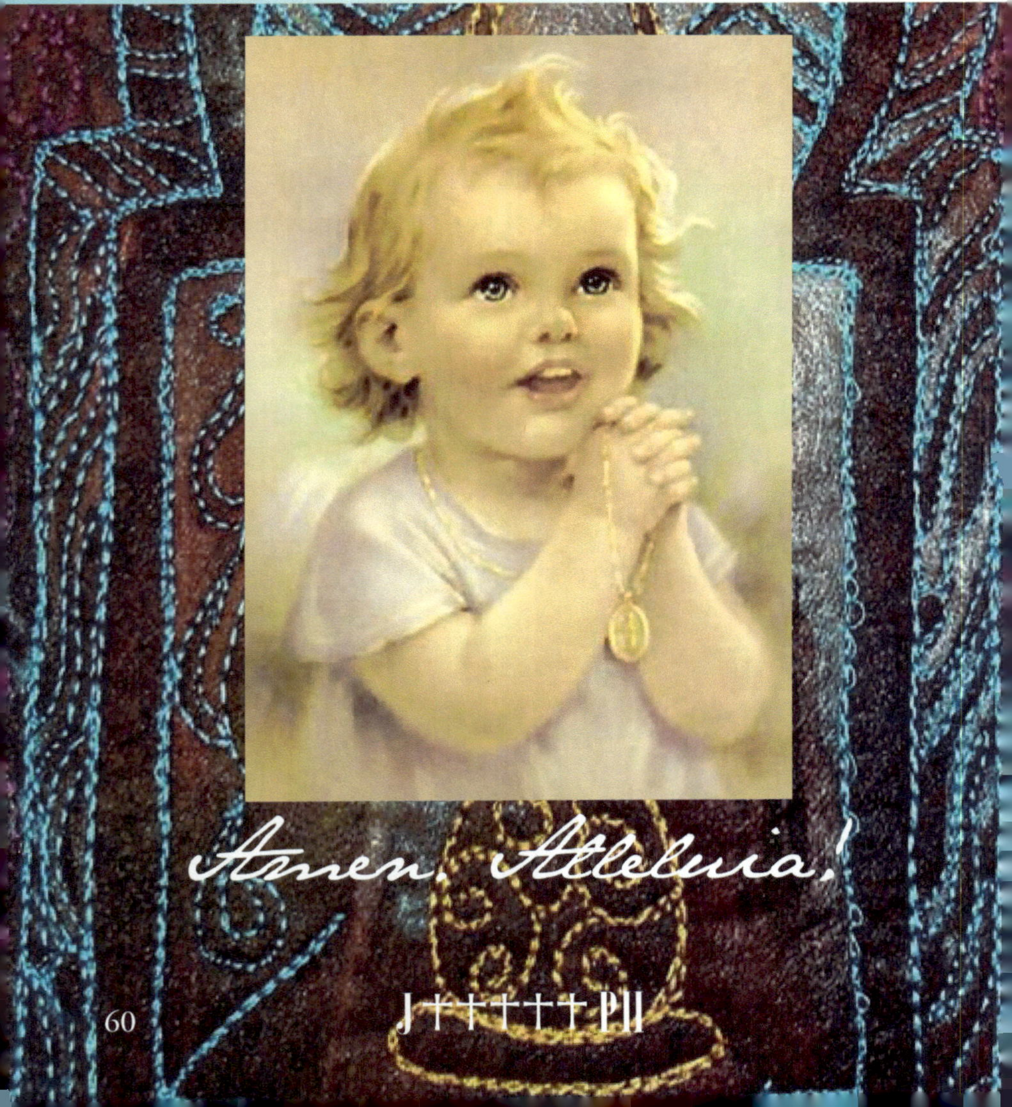

23
THE HOLY POPE SPEAKS *Saint John Paul II*

My children, listen to me well, very well. Today I wish you to focus on the purity and whiteness of your soul before God.

What is the state of your soul? Have you admitted and confessed your sins before God recently? Have you done an extensive review of all your thoughts and committed actions that were not perfectly holy in the Eyes of God?

I say unto you, I say unto you verily, there is little time ahead of you to cleanse your soul of impurities accumulated over the years and to atone for your sins.

I strongly recommend that you read the book entitled *Saint Padre Pio Speaks* and that you go to confession with a priest of your parish, and this, as soon as possible, and regularly. For time is short and the purification of your soul is urgently required so as to progress quickly on your path of return to God—especially if you desire to appear before Him in a state of Holiness!

Alleluia! Alleluia! Alleluia!
Blessed is he who submits regularly
to the Sacred Sacrament of Confession
for in this God truly rejoices.

Amen. Alleluia!

24 THE HOLY POPE SPEAKS — Saint John Paul II

My children, listen to me well once more. The destiny of your soul is not decided tomorrow or in any future. It is decided now! Be prepared to hear Christ Jesus knocking at your door, the door of your heart, today! For tomorrow belongs to God and God decides everything, concerning everything and at all times, on earth as in Heaven.

Alleluia! Alleluia! Alleluia!
Blessed is he who prepares himself today,
for today this one shall be saved.

Amen. Alleluia!

THE HOLY POPE SPEAKS: Saint John Paul II

My children, I am delighted to meet you now through this book blessed by God. When I was Pope, I wanted to meet the entire world! My interest and my compassion for each and every human being has prompted me to travel a great deal and to plan several meetings with men, women, and children worldwide. What a pleasure to discover the personalities of everyone that God had sent me during my Papacy! Such sadness to notice the states of human souls wandering the earth…

For this reason, I take particular interest in knowing you, dear reader, to get closer to you, to understand your inner dynamics, your strengths and weaknesses, your qualities and your flaws, all the problems and dramas of your life, in order to help you and assist you in a Divine Way, that is to say, completely, perfectly, and miraculously.

THE HOLY POPE SPEAKS — Saint John Paul II

I say unto you, I say unto you verily, I know you now better than I could have known you before, when I was Pope John Paul II, and my assistance in your life is, at this point in your life, and will become as of now, much more important than you can imagine. For my Holiness is with you, dear precious soul, and my Holiness is part of the Light of Christ, by the Grace of the Living God.

Alleluia! Alleluia! Alleluia!
Blessed is he who lives his life assisted by the Holiness of Saint John Paul II, for the Light of Christ is with him, now and for eternity.

ANGELUS DOMINI DESCENDIT DE CŒLO ET ACCEDENS REVOLVIT LAPIDEM ET SEDEBAT

69

THE HOLY POPE SPEAKS — Saint John Paul II

My children,

I hasten to tell you a story. When I was a young man living in Poland with my father, I was quite intrigued by human suffering and the source of evil afflicting man.

One day, when I was walking on the street, meditating on the deep meaning of life on earth, a vision appeared before me: suddenly, an Angel materialized! A beautiful Angel, very tall, quite illuminated, with white and silky wings, of perfect and magnificent beauty!

I was shocked and astounded, but I was not afraid. He told me that He was my Guardian Angel, and that He had been authorized by God to manifest Himself to me in the physical plane. In addition, He said He would protect me and guide me always, through all the trials of my life, and that I should pray to Him often. He made me promise not to share this vision with anyone during my life on earth, and then He disappeared. What a shock! Such joy! Such feeling of infinite protection!

THE HOLY POPE SPEAKS

That is my Message today, dear reader. Your soul is in my hands, in the Hands of Saint Paul, the Master Jesus, the Virgin Mary, the Holy Spirit, your Guardian Angel, and especially in the wise and loving Hands of God the Father Almighty, your Creator.

Be not afraid! I have said it before and I will say it again: be not afraid! For your precious soul is protected from the enemy's wickedness.

Alleluia! Alleluia! Alleluia!
Blessed is he who believes in his Guardian Angel
and prays to Him
for infinite protection is assured him.

Amen. Alleluia!

THE HOLY POPE SPEAKS Saint John Paul II

My children, my children, let me speak to you about your Guardian Angel.

The intimate experience I had with my Guardian Angel when I lived on earth has been a profound revelation for me. My promise to my Angel was kept and I have never revealed to anyone this extraordinary event of my life. That is why historians, journalists, and writers have never reported this Mystical and personal experience.

However, I can assure you that not a day of my life went by, as a result of my supernatural meeting, during which I did not think of or pray to my Angel, this grandiose Blessing of Divine Providence.

My Guardian Angel has performed countless miracles for me, including rescuing me from the assassination attempt of 1981 and other incidents that have more or less infiltrated the press. My many travels, my meeting with thousands of individuals, and my Parkinson's disease at the end of my life, made me vulnerable to the assaults of the enemy. Fortunately, Glory be to God, an infinite protection shielded me from the numerous threats surrounding me.

THE HOLY POPE SPEAKS: Saint John Paul II

Your Guardian Angel helps you and loves you and He is always at your side. When I behold you, dear child, I can see a beautiful smile of joy and gratitude on His Angelic Face! For your soul is bathed in the Christic Light, the fruit of Divine Mercy on your soul and, thanks to our Divine intercessions, that of your Angel and of your humble servant in Heaven, Saint John Paul II, who loves you!

*Alleluia! Alleluia! Alleluia!
Blessed is he who awakens to the Blessing
of the Guardian Angel,
for this Blessing will flourish even further.*

Amen. Alleluia!

J ☩ ☩ ☩ ☩ ☩ PII

THE HOLY POPE SPEAKS — Saint John Paul II

My children,

I am delighted that God has chosen you to be part of the Legion of Saint Paul at this time of your life. From now on, your Mystical and Spiritual development will be accelerated and obstacles and delays that were blocking your way in the past will be eliminated. Such joy in Heaven when a beautiful soul radiates the Light of Christ! Such pleasure for the Father, our Creator, to see one of His children hasten into His loving Arms! For God the Father is waiting for you all, and He has reserved a Particular and Infinite Mercy to the members of the Legion of Saint Paul.

*Alleluia! Alleluia! Alleluia!
Blessed are the members of the Legion of Saint Paul,
for God Himself reaches out to them.*

Amen. Alleluia!

29

THE HOLY POPE SPEAKS — Saint John Paul II

My children,

I am enchanted to be part of the Legion of Saint Paul, as are all those who live here in Paradise. Soon you will also understand the extraordinary merits that the Soul of Saint Paul has acquired, 2,000 years ago and since.

The Soul of Saint Paul is the Logos of conversion to Christ Jesus. This means that His Soul derives directly from the Central Sun, the Divine Fire at the origin of the Creation, according to the Will of the Father Almighty. The Logos of Saint Paul represents a Sphere of Transcendent and Mystical Teaching in what concerns the true Knowledge of God and His Creation.

The Logos of Saint Paul vibrates throughout the universe, through dimensions known and unknown to man. In fact, your heart contains the Logos of Saint Paul despite your lack of awakening to its fundamental Teaching. When you awaken to the Presence of Christ in your life, it produces within you several phenomena Mystical and salutary to the soul. Among these phenomena is written the awakening of the Logos of Saint Paul and the pouring forth in your heart of a more elevated and illuminated understanding of what God is, and of Christ, His Only Son, through the operations of the Holy Spirit.

THE HOLY POPE SPEAKS Saint John Paul II

Subsequently, the progressive awakening of your Consciousness in relation to the Teaching of Saint Paul the Apostle opens the door to your royal entry into the Legion of Saint Paul. This critical step in your life is extraordinary, for the Infinite and Ineffable Mercy of God is granted to you by virtue of the merits gained by the Soul of Saint Paul during the history of humanity.

Alleluia! Alleluia! Alleluia!
Blessed is the Soul of Saint Paul,
the Logos of conversion to Christ,
the Symbol of Infinite Mercy
written in your heart forever.

Amen. Alleluia!

THE HOLY POPE SPEAKS Saint John Paul II

My children, being part of the Legion of Saint Paul signifies your initiation on the path of redemption. This path is narrow, winding, and strewn with obstacles, but it takes you directly to the Kingdom of God, where I live with the other Saints in Paradise and the Angels of God.

The Legion of Saint Paul is symbolized by the five crosses for the following reason: the number five incorporates the Transcendental Knowledge of Laws and Principles of the universe as created by God. The cross represents the sacrifice made by Christ and all the Saints in Heaven in order to expiate the sins committed against God and men.

The five crosses thus symbolize and enclose a unique and extraordinary process of redemption gained by the Soul of Saint Paul, Master Servant of God, and they grant Infinite Mercy to your precious soul, dear reader, by the Grace and the Will of the Loving and Living God.

O blessed be the Soul of the Saint Paul the Apostle! O let us give Glory to God for such Mercy!

THE HOLY POPE SPEAKS: Saint John Paul II

Hasten to say Yes and to agree to become a member of the Legion of Saint Paul. Simply say: "My Father, my Creator, I thank you for helping my suffering soul of a sinner; pull me from the abyss of the misery of the world and save me by your Power. Today I wish to become a member of the Legion of Saint Paul and obtain thereby the Blessing and Mercy enclosed within the five crosses. I pray to you and I thank you, by the Precious Blood of our Lord Jesus Christ, your Only Son, and the Immaculate Heart of Mary. Amen."

Alleluia!

J ✝ ✝ ✝ ✝ ✝ P II

31 THE HOLY POPE SPEAKS: Saint John Paul II

My children,
I will speak to you a little more about my childhood. My father was very pious. After the death of my poor mother, my father was even more immersed in prayer, in order to protect us, him and me, from further dramas. His death, when I was twenty-one, deeply troubled me. My soul had become lonely among men of the earth.

I then decided that my family would henceforth be of Heavenly Origin: my Divine Mother became the Blessed Virgin Mary and my Divine Father became God the Father Almighty. Christ Jesus, my Savior and my God, became my Cosmic Friend, my Miraculous Brother, my Bridge to the afterlife, my Master and my King.

My Family was always with me wherever I went, no matter what I was doing or the state of my soul. My Heavenly Family and I were always united, always working, always in a state of prayer, always in the accomplishment of Divine Justice, and always bathed in Divine Love.

Alleluia! Alleluia! Alleluia!
Blessed is he who adopts the Heavenly Family in his life,
for Divine Blessings are always with him.

Amen. Alleluia!

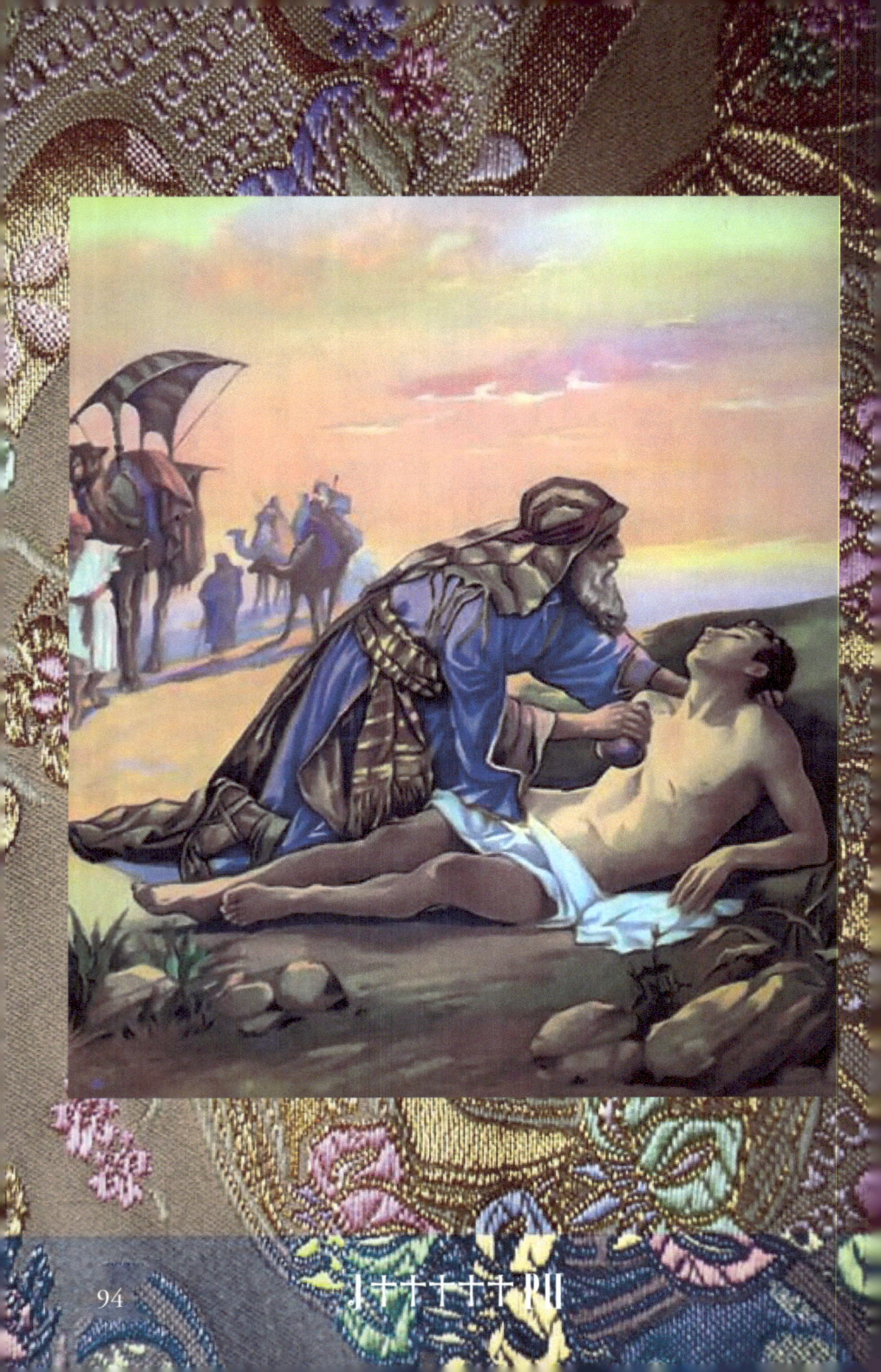

THE HOLY POPE SPEAKS — Saint John Paul II

My children,
I am here above in Heaven and I behold you with all the Divine Compassion held in Paradise. I have obtained the Gift of Holiness by the Ineffable Grace of the Living God. I have also obtained the Gift of Compassion by the same Grace.

Consequently, my role in your life is played on two levels: I desire to present you in a state of Holiness before God the Father Almighty after the passage that is death. Just as equally, I also desire to instruct you and ennoble you with the Grace of Compassion, a virtue that pleases the Father through the merits and the good deeds which result among men on earth.

For my compassion for mankind has dominated my Papacy, it is true, but above all compassion has moved my heart which has swelled with love, solicitude, and charity toward my fellowmen. For compassion opens the door to many other virtues, enriching the heart and elevating the soul toward God.

Alleluia! Alleluia! Alleluia!
Blessed are the hearts of compassion, for the Gift
of Compassion is a Grace given by God Himself
in order to elevate the soul toward Him.

Amen. Alleluia!

33 — THE HOLY POPE SPEAKS: Saint John Paul II

My children,

I am pleased to speak to you about my childhood. I was very close to my mother; when she died, I was devastated, confused, fragmented. I did not know to whom to give my heart.

My mother taught me the fundamental principles of the Catechism at an early age. My mother was as beautiful and miraculous, in my eyes, as the Most Blessed Virgin Mary. Consequently, after her painful death, I gave all my heart, all my life, and all my soul to my new Mother, the Most Beautiful, Most Holy, Most Wonderful Virgin Mary. She has been there next to me all my life, and She has watched over me during my Pontificate with Infinite Tenderness and Infinite Mercy. For our Divine Mother, the Most Blessed Virgin Mary, is indivisible from Her Son, our Lord Jesus Christ, our Savior.

When you pray to the Virgin Mary, you pray also and just as equally to Christ Jesus; and when you pray to Christ Jesus, the Virgin Mary, consequently, receives the same prayers in all Her Benevolence. Do you see? The Mother is Co-Redeemer with the Son; for God the Father has decided so at the beginning of the Creation.

THE HOLY POPE SPEAKS: Saint John Paul II

I implore you, my dear children: say your rosary every day, and pray to your Good Mother, our Divine Mother of all, the Most Blessed Virgin Mary, and you will be showered with unexpected miracles.

Alleluia! Alleluia! Alleluia!
Blessed be the Mother of God,
our Divine Mother, by virtue of
Her Miraculous and Redemptive Powers.

Amen. Alleluia!

J ✝ ✝ ✝ ✝ ✝ PII

34 THE HOLY POPE SPEAKS Saint John Paul II

My children, I wish to speak to you today about my Pontificate. I was in a state of elation and happiness without precedent in my life when the committee elected me Pope in 1978. My inner Spiritual life, which had expanded and had been enriched by the adoption of my Heavenly Family, as you know, redoubled with zeal, intensity, and devotion for God the Father Almighty for such Mercy on my soul.

I am a servant of God now, of course, but I also was at the time, because I had developed an intimate and unique relationship with God the Father. I knew in the depths of my heart that God the Father Almighty loved me, supported me, and presented me with hundreds of opportunities to serve Him, to please Him, and to bear witness to His Sovereign Presence throughout everything and at all times. My personal devotion to God the Father, as a human soul walking on earth and as Pontiff of the Catholic people, was genuine and total for Him, our Creator of all.

THE HOLY POPE SPEAKS: Saint John Paul II

I wish to convey and teach you the same degree of devotion that I experienced as a man. Pray! Pray! Pray! Abandon yourself to God, the One Who created you, and you will obtain His Divine Mercy in your life. For God the Father loves you and desires only your happiness on earth.

Alleluia! Alleluia! Alleluia!
Blessed is he who offers himself to God,
for God Himself will give him
His Divine Blessings.

Amen. Alleluia!

35 THE HOLY POPE SPEAKS — Saint John Paul II

My beloved children, I wish to speak to you today about your soul as well as mine.

When I was a child in Poland, I did not suspect the importance of a healthy soul. However, my mother, before she died, and my father, during most of my youth, were preoccupied with the health of my soul. They instructed me in the foundations of Catechism, they took me to Mass, they taught me religious rituals to practice at home and in my spare time. As an obedient child, I put into practice the commands received from my parents, and consequently, I took care of the health of my soul, through the Divine Grace of God who touched my soul from an early age.

Therefore, my beloved children, I implore you from the bottom of my heart: take care of the health of your soul. Today, fill your day, blessed by God, with all kinds of holy elements: place religious relics around your home, wear a cross on your neck, say prayers in the morning, midday and at night, say your rosary every day, go to Mass as often as possible, read the Bible and other religious materials that the Holy Spirit will put on your path, and build an inner life solely centered on God the Father Almighty.

THE HOLY POPE SPEAKS — Saint John Paul II

Shortly, very shortly, innumerable Blessings and Miracles will transform your life, for God the Father is reaching out to you today, through the luminous book you are holding in your hands, and which will guide your steps toward Him, our Creator, with my Holy assistance.

Alleluia! Alleluia! Alleluia!
Blessed is he who takes care of his soul,
for God the Father Himself will take care of that soul.

Amen. Alleluia!

J ✝ ✝ ✝ ✝ ✝ PII

THE HOLY POPE SPEAKS — Saint John Paul II

My children,

I wish to speak to you about Parkinson's disease, which has afflicted me at the end of my life. This suffering, coupled with a degree of humiliation before the Catholic people owing to my inability to perform the full scope of my Apostolic and Papal mission, has performed a final and radical transformation of my soul before God.

In this way, I paid the debt I owed to God, which went back to the time of my youth. I intensified my intimate prayers to God in order to ask His Mercy on my soul, and I surrendered myself completely to His Hands of Love. The result was the glorious and full redemption of my soul and of my Spirit in His Eyes immediately before my physical death, which, although dramatic, was necessary in the Eyes of God.

You see, therefore, the necessity and value of suffering in the Eyes of God? God Himself decides the precise degree of suffering He prescribes to your soul in order to purify it and make it beautiful and white as snow at the moment of passage that is death.

THE HOLY POPE SPEAKS — Saint John Paul II

Never doubt the Cosmic Plan of God concerning your life and be not afraid to suffer a little—or a little more—for Him. For He sees everything, He feels everything, and He knows exactly what you are experiencing, each and every one of you, at every moment of your life.

Alleluia! Alleluia! Alleluia!
Blessed is he who suffers,
for this one moves closer to God
according to His Supreme Will.

Amen. Alleluia!

J ✝✝✝✝✝ PII

THE HOLY POPE SPEAKS — Saint John Paul II

My children, I wish to speak to you today about your future life. I do not refer to life on earth, oh no! I refer to life in the Great Beyond, life in the Kingdom of God awaiting you if you continue your Spiritual work on your path of return toward God.

I promise my Holy and Heavenly assistance to you, dear reader, dear soul in distress, dear precious soul in the Eyes of God. For God is present in all His children and He desires to see each and everyone of you return peacefully home, His Home, the Kingdom of Heaven. Soon, we will all be here, reunited in the Kingdom, all the Father's children having returned to the shelter in the House of the Father, flooded in Christic Light, enlightened by the Knowledge of the Holy Spirit, and bathed in the Love of the Father.

For the Father loves you so much... Oh! He loves you so much!

Alleluia! Alleluia! Alleluia!
Blessed is he who makes the decision today
to return to the Father's House,
for the Father Himself in this rejoices.

Amen. Alleluia!

THE HOLY POPE SPEAKS Saint John Paul II

My children, I am concluding my Divine Teaching today. The Kingdom of God is awaiting you, I repeat it unto you. I will be at the Door of the Kingdom to greet you, to embrace you, and to apply on your forehead your Cross of Holiness.

Invoke me often. Say: "Saint John Paul II, intercede for me, before God the Father Almighty, for the obtention of the Grace of Holiness and the Grace of Compassion, by virtue of your Gift of Holiness and your Gift of Compassion, in the Holy Name of our Savior Jesus Christ and the Immaculate Heart of Mary. Amen."

Be strong and courageous before the events that lie ahead, pray without ceasing, read and read again the holy book you are holding in your hands, read all the books published in this collection, for these books, received in dictation by Marie-Josée T., the essence of Saint Paul on earth, are blessed by God Himself, and put into practice all the lessons received. And of all this, God the Father will rejoice, and will offer you His Infinite Mercy, by virtue of the merits won by the five crosses.

I bless you in the Name of the Father, and of the Son, and of the Holy Spirit. Amen!

I love you.

Saint John Paul II
Karol Wojtyla

AFTERWORD

Saint John Paul II stood by your side as you were reading this book. Did you feel his presence?

He said, "Saint John Paul II, the Pope you have known and loved and in whom you have put all your trust and all your hope, will never abandon you. I promise you. I am Saint John Paul II, and I love you."

What a beautiful and powerful message! Be not afraid!

Saint John Paul II, I love you!

Marie-Josée

ABOUT THE AUTHOR

Marie-Josée Thibault's life is in no way similar to yours. When she wakes, the saints of Heaven visit her, talk to her, teach her, and pray intensely with her. When such mystical sessions draw to a close, she greets with great respect and deep reverence the Masters of the Heavenly Court. This servant of the Lord spends the rest of the day in the company of her guardian angel, who continues her spiritual education and ceaselessly protects her from the perils of this fallen world.

Bestowed by the Heavenly Father, her gifts of clairvoyance and clairaudience allow her to remain in continuous contact with the supernatural dimension juxtaposed with ours, where the soul is born of the Spirit through Jesus and Mary. She prays that, one day soon, the entire human race will give glory to the Father, the Son, and the Holy Spirit.

ALSO BY THE AUTHOR

- Saint Padre Pio Speaks: Book 1
- Abba, Your Father, Speaks: Book I
- Abba, Your Father, Speaks: Book II
- Angel Gabriel Speaks: Book 1
- Saint Beethoven Speaks: Book 1
- Saint Bernadette Speaks Book 1
- Dear Humanity: Book 1
- Dear Humanity: Book 2
- Saint Therese of Lisieux Speaks: Book 1
- Saint Joan of Arc Speaks
- Saint Martin de Porres Speaks - Book 1
- Saint Barnabas Speaks: Book 1

Pray, my children, pray again!

~ Saint John Paul II

Saint John Paul II
Karol Wojtyla
(1920-2005)

FREE DOWNLOAD

Get your free copy of:
"Saint Padre Pio Speaks: Book 1" when you sign up to the author's VIP mailing list! Get started here:

www.abbamyfatheriloveyou.com

www.ingramcontent.com/pod-product-compliance
Lightning Source LLC
Chambersburg PA
CBHW042218240426
43670CB00034B/12